CHANGE

— THE —

World

EDITED BY

JENNI HARRISON

First published in Great Britain in 2018 by:

Forward Poetry

Remus House
Coltsfoot Drive
Peterborough
PE2 9BF
Telephone: 01733 890099
Website: www.forwardpoetry.co.uk

FOREWORD

Here at Forward Poetry we pride ourselves on supplying inspiring themes to encourage creative, poetic minds, and then providing the bridge to publication and a wider audience for their poetry once they put pen to paper.

For our latest anthology, inspired by World Environment Day on 5th June, we invited writers to submit a poem on the subject of the ever-changing natural world around them. This is a beautiful collection of work, reflective and insightful, which you are sure to enjoy revisiting time and time again.

We are very proud to present this anthology and we are sure it will provide entertainment and inspiration for years to come.

To. Janet
Love, Lorna x

CONTENTS

THE POEMS

CHANGING THE WORLD?

Change the world they said
Mate, you need to ditch the big head
You're no better because you don't eat meat
Or because you want to bomb the Middle East
You're no better because of the party you vote
Or because of the university that you go to
You're no better because of a verse or two
And it makes no difference the job you do
The world won't change while opinions fly
While we fight over political and media lies
And if the world does change it'll be of benefit to the rich
Do you think they give a shit?
We're too busy fighting over petty news
Scraping over political views
We talk about saving trees while bombing kids
We ignore world events whole talking TOWIE and bimbos' cribs
We give to charities with directors on wages
More than all ours combined
Yet when we see someone homeless it's too much to be kind
And you hate me because I want to change the world
But don't vote Green
Call it arrogance but the problem ain't me
I see in all directions, all walks of life
Maybe you should give it a try
The world won't change when you won't lend an ear
How else do you think we all ended up here?

Regan Roberts

FOR THE LOVE OF HONEY

Today I met a honeybee.
This is the story she told to me.

"Humans, we know you.
For thousands of years we have known you.
We have lived by you.
Around you. With you.
You have plundered our sacred stores.
We have garnered knowledge of your wily mores.
We learned to defend our regal abode.
With a poison that we perish to unload.
But still you watch us with hungry eyes.
Eager for the golden prize.

Your generations move far slower than ours.
And we pass on the ways of our Aparian lores.
Evolution moved and you tried to tame us.
Keep us, know us, rule us, own us.
You marvelled at our anatomical form.
As closer you studied how we were born.
How we live and work and breed.
Communicate, think, forage and feed.
You thought, by right, you would know it all.
From birth to death, our rise and fall.

Two breeds of Man developed to know us.
Those who cared and strived to help us.
And those that wanted nothing but honey.
Alchemists, turning nectar to honey.
Education, knowledge of our way of being.

Is there for those who have a way of seeing.
Be not the humans who take us for granted.
Regarding our kind as just insects unwanted.
We are precious, needy, vital.
Transient in our living cycle.

Communing with flora is our reason to be.
Field or garden; every flower, every tree.
Garnering fare for our proliferation.
For the advancement of our insect nation.
Care for us if it pleases your kind
And observe us with an open mind.
Be kind, be patient with understanding.
Learn of our ways with careful handling.
Pray to Saint Ambrose for favourable times
And keep us in most temperate climes.

We are an ancient, wandering race.
From the tropical forests to this often cold place.
We long existed before the ascent of Man.
With his domineering, god-like plan.
Alas! You need us.
Cannot live without us.
Pollination brings your precious food.
Perhaps we are symbiotic, you and I.
So look beyond your own mind's eye.

Curb your ways of deforestation.
Cutting, mowing, defoliation.
Leave for us Flora's abundant bounty.
Full of sweet nectar among its beauty.
We are Apis mellifera, the honeybee.

Most precious of all insects flying free.
Destined to live beyond the annals of Man.
Think of our kind, whilst ever you can.
Humans, we know you.
So to us be true."

Today I met a honeybee.
And I love honey, sweet as can be.
For I would miss this unctuous treat.
'Food of the gods'; better yet to meet.
So too, many foods we want, nay! Need.
Help to save this industrious breed.
If they were gone, lost forever in time
So we would follow, in 'rhythm and rhyme'.

Margaret Edge

UNTITLED

As the sea surges, we blame it for surging.
As the climate differs, we blame it for differing.
As natural disasters take a dramatic turn,
we blame it for occurring.
Rather than blaming Mother Nature and its natural resources,
we should stitch our hearts together.
Come to a settlement and fight to make a sentimental difference
in a world that needs a source of harmony.
We appreciate the work of the governments. We really do.
When one individual alters the world,
this individual cannot do it alone.
The rest of the world is on that individual's case to intervene
and support that individual,
as the town halls play a symphony where rainforests
and all the greenery call for a collective change
in the plight of intolerable terrorism, cultural differences,
social norms and disputes spotted by the people in our society.
Oh people of our society, commit to a lifetime change in this world
and open our eyes to irreplaceable love
you will plant in your heart for those
from a contrasting religion and heritage.
If you won't commit, then question your ideologies
and thesis or yourself;
Who will commit to this inevitable change in the world!

Redwan Ahmed

SCIENCE THE SAVIOUR, EARTH THE DYING

For millennia we have survived,
For millennia we have died,
Forever we have desired knowledge.
And forever knowledge is waiting.
And forever we have had it, no matter the cost.

We are contempt in our leader's cold embrace,
In our destruction of this good Earth,
But instead, what we desire is the cold of space,
And a new, better Earth.

Yesterday industry breath...
Today worldly death.
Destruction is in our culture.
But so is redemption and change.

A world among the stars.
A people almost united in the quest for Mars.
And yet we can't see past our own destruction.
People of all race and creed,
United by the goal of knowledge,
By the cold realisation of our scale,
And by the warm realisation of our destiny.
That's the hope, that's the dream.
To not try is to fail,
But to try, to fail, to succeed - that's the human identity.

We are united by
The promise of freedom.

Freedom from tyranny,
Freedom from a world tearing itself apart
And taking everyone and everything with it.
A new beginning for our species, our planet...

Interstellar humans,
Traversing the stars.
Reversing our mistakes.
Seeking peace and prosperity,
With caution and solidarity.

Humanity United,
Under the banner of inspiration ignited.
Finally, we see our mistakes,
Finally, we slam the brakes,
And start the repairs.

Humans beyond Earth,
Mankind travelling beyond dreams,
The dreams of generations,
To travel the galaxy...
And return to a safe home.

Space will change our view of the world,
It will change our priorities and our plans.
It makes us look inward.
To our planet, not just the stars.
To what we do, our actions and responsibilities,
Space shows us we are unique.
It shows us our past greed,
And that one day we will be tried,
Because of our actions on this planet.

But partly through space, we can be freed.
Space shows our future unity truly agreed.

We've worked, still work and forever will work,
Despite the obstacles,
Without help from the crop circles,
We work in common cause,
For our future, our future's future, and beyond,
To clear our mess,
To leave no regret,
And forge a path to the stars.

Ad Astra et Retro

Josh Perkins

CHANGE THE WORLD

A Christian went into a mosque to pray
A Muslim sat in a church on a sunny day
Children that wept
But now they have slept
Wake from their slumber
Everyone is a number
The planet is creaking and groaning with pain
And all because Man wants to gain
Kingdoms and palaces, leaders and lands
But we are destroying the beauty made with God's loving hands
We are merely mortals, only visitors here
The pleas of the nations are falling on deaf ears
The lion will walk beside the lamb
The flood waters will stop at the foot of the dam
Roses will bloom in the mid-winter snow
All of the creatures will have somewhere to go
The stars and the moon will be the only light
Apart from the sun shining so bright
Birdsong, the cuckoo, the lark and the dove
The seas and the rivers sent from Heaven above
Guns will be melted, swords thrown away
As the world rejoices at the break of a new day
With no threat of violence, revenge or regret
This could be reality... it's not over yet
So let's change the world
Everyone, you and me
And let's just delight... in each other's company.
This is my dream.

Dorothy Kay

STOP AND LISTEN FOR EARTH

As you go about the hustle and bustle of life,
Have you ever stopped to think about the planet's strife?
Probably not: we're all busy making money,
To make ends meet and make sure no one goes hungry.
When actually there are some of us who do,
And though we try to believe it is untrue,
But it is.
As those less fortunate struggle to survive,
Our planet no longer feels alive.

Have you ever stopped and listened
Or watched the water glisten?
Heard the creaking of the crickets
Or the buzzing of bugs in the thickets?
Watched the mighty eagle dive
As the fish in the water come alive?
Tasted the salt by the sea
As you eat an ice cream, two or three?
Sat on top of a hill so high
That you are almost touching the sky?
Stood on top of a cliff and bellow,
So you can hear your echo in the valley below?
Dipped your toes into the fast-flowing stream
Like you would see in a dream?
Seen the little blackbird build a nest
In the high and thick canopy of the forest?
Or even seen a duck waddle along,
Like its cousin the penguin, where in the Antarctic it belongs?
Seen flowers bloom so bright

They are not shaded by the darkness of the night?
Or seen the big eyes of a deer,
Who just as quickly disappeared?

For those of you more travelled,
Have you ever seen a meteor shower?
Or seen the performance of the Northern Lights
Under the blanket of snow and ice?
Those of you who take interest in the past
Seen the Pyramids, the Colosseum and the Taj Mahal?
Those of you who like to climb,
Seen Kilimanjaro, Himalayas and views so sublime?
Or those of you who like to roam,
Or techies who see the views from a drone.
Have you ever just stopped and looked,
And maybe seen the dip of a tiny little babbling brook?

If you've answered 'yes' to any of these,
Then I need to beg you please;
Though we are admiring the endless cosmos above,
We are forgetting the one thing that we should love:
Our planet, Earth.
It holds a beauty envied by many,
But it is being destroyed by plenty
Of things that did not exist billions of years ago:
Before Earth's tale ends in woe,
Let us team together to make our home planet glow.

Rachel Maisey

THIS ONCE BLUE WORLD

(The Year 12017)

Once there were beings that dwelled on this Earth
Every land mass and ocean supported their birth
They lived on this planet, strived to reach out to space
But to run before walking brought an end to their race

Earth's early days were gentle of ways
Man lived off the fruits of the land
Then came the desire for flesh on the fire
They had spears, they had arrows to hand
Nothing was sacred and little was safe
They would kill just for pleasure and blood
Then came the tribes and then came the nations
And then came a terrible flood

One man was brave and his family was saved
They rode out the terrible storm
Their ark beached on sand close to mountainous land
Where the legend of Noah was born
Noah saved all the animals, setting them free
A fresh chance to open new doors
But the spirit of Man then said 'take all we can'
And the killing resumed as before

They would kill in their cities, they would kill in their towns
They would sacrifice all sent their way
Theatres of death were built all around
Blood soaked the sand and the clay
They murdered their leaders, they crucified God
As he tried to bring love to their towns

And then came the guns, the bullets, the wars
Then came the steep pathway down

They destroyed one another, their sisters and brothers
They destroyed every nation and land
Where once there were valleys verdant and green
They changed them to desert and sand
Pollution then stripped out what Man failed to kill
Until nothing that lived could remain
Just the memory of a once blue and beautiful world
And I wonder!
Can nature rebuild it again?

Because once there were beings that dwelled on this Earth
Every land mass and ocean supported their birth
They lived on this planet, strived to reach out to space
But their violent nature spelled the end of their race.

Keith Nuhrenburg-Wilson

CHILD'S WAR

Every time I turn my head,
A new war has begun,
They say it's for the good of Man,
But how, when there's people dying,
They say it's about peace,
Yet it just causes more wars,
They say it's to save people,
But there are men and women dying.

They say it's to save a country,
And all of its people,
They say it's for the good of Man,
But these are just all lies,
They think that war's a game,
It's a child's war,
But these guns are real,
These gory deaths toll up,
When will they see
This isn't a child's war?

They say,
They just want world peace,
Well I say,
How do they expect to get it?
Through violence and exploits,
I think,
We should have our say
Before it's too late.

They say it's to save a country,
And all of its people,
They say it's for the good of Man,
But these are just all lies,
They think that war's a game,
It's a child's war,
But these guns are real,
These gory deaths toll up,
When will they see
This isn't a child's war?

But if you think
How many people are saved?
In a ratio to how many die?
You may start to think
War isn't bad at all,
I mean yeah,
There's people dying,
And yeah,
The cost of war is high,
But isn't it worth it to save
A few thousand people,
And eventually,
End up saving the world?

They say it's to save a country,
And all of its people,
They say it's for the good of Man,
But these are just all lies,
They think that war's a game,
It's a child's war,

But these guns are real,
These gory deaths toll up,
When will they see
This isn't a child's war?

Daniel Greenhalgh

AUTUMN MOSSES, SPRING MORES

The birches seem dreamlike, and below
a pale, wan sun gives most fragile light
across the reed bed of stilled feathery heads
that is the moss in late year

We slowly chill, as cloudfall makes it seem any
month's fill-dyke, though this year it's been unearthly dry
and the lake's in grey retreat; in summer the oaks
massive, ebullient, boast their vibrant greenery
to azure sky, as if Titian himself:
the greatest painter of sun-blued sky
waits for for the new year's inspiration

But now it's the moss itself that calls
damp-dank, echoing centuries' decay and yet
rebirth; we think of it, this day, alcoholically
speeding empty roads, and ribaldry...

'A saloon is where I feel most at home'
which western did I take that from? Who cares?
We all, there, fitful sun on inglenooked chair backs or
closeted in comfy shade feel the call
to spring-focus'd bonhomie

to toasting each other and the atmosphere:
gleam of glass, treat of taste
thoughts race from here to bursting bulbs
loosened leaves, combustive colours and
'to the next time!'

Christopher Brookes

PRECIOUS PLANET

The seasons do not appear to be as they were anymore
Not sure if it's climate change or a cosmic flaw
There is so much that we do not understand
Whether it be in the air or sea or land
We adapt without even knowing at times
Only worry when there are unusual signs
These alert us and make us question the cause
We live in very unstable times as there are conflicts and wars
This impacts on us as a nation, it is true to say
I can confirm at present night still follows day
You do wonder at the power of atmospheric change
Does it affect people and make them act strange?
The sun is very powerful, not only with its heat
It can influence our demeanour by making life appear sweet
Who is to blame you may ask, 'H' is the clue letter
Yes humans who should and do know better
Carelessly destroying to achieve their own aim
This selfish behaviour has only short-term gain
'Live for today' you hear many people say
Sadly there will be no tomorrow, for many who get in their way
These people with no morals, are they missing a gene?
They act so ruthless giving no thought to what there's been
Responsibility for one's actions should always be taught
Understand all in life is precious,
As a clear conscience can't be bought
We all want a future so companies and countries should think
Otherwise the big picture could be gone in a wink
To raise awareness of our delicate planet is the only hope
The young will be our saviours, saving us from the slippery slope

Teach them to question and not accept what is said
Search for solutions as our futures are in their head
They will deliver as they have knowledge and flair
Our part is always to show love and to care.

Anne Sackey

ABC OF CLIMATE CHANGE

A ccumulation of greenhouse gases in the atmosphere.

B urning of fossil fuels and rainforests are also vanishing.

C reating significant climate change round the biosphere.

D isappearing Arctic ice and more powerful waves approaching.

E ternal energy is wind, tidal and solar power.

F ood and farm animals are also immense climate changers.

G reenhouse effect forbids the planet to blossom and flower.

H eatwaves, drought, and heavy rain result in major weather dangers.

I mpact of climate change is occurring at maximum speed.

J oin Greenpeace in the quest to protect the environment worldwide.

K eep pollution levels down and global peace will be achieved.

L oss and damages from the extreme weather changes will subside.

M an's lure of the digital age is a new contributor.

N itrous oxide participates in global warming is also true.

O ceans absorbing CO_2 is an important x-factor.

P aris Agreement states keep Earth's temperature rise below 2°C; Trump should too.

Q UELRO targets must be achieved by all developed nations.

R eproduction of organisms needs correct environments.

S ea level rises affects both wildlife and coastal stations.

T hese adaptions occur slowly, sneakily and in silence.

U NFCCC stops unsafe human intrusion of the climate system.

V ulnerability influences the talents to survive.

W e must change our carbon footprints for the right ecosystem.

X shows we are not achieving the required levels to thrive.

Y ou must act immediately and take up obligation.

Z ero carbon transport and homes must be on the legislation.

Inderjeet Deusi

UNTITLED

I'd love to make the world a happier place
Putting a smile on every single face
Washing badness away with every tide
Giving evil beings nowhere to hide
We would all forget how to judge
And would banish bullies with just a nudge
We'd welcome everyone without alarm
Knowing no one on Earth could cause us harm
This would help us make the right choices
Getting things done with just our voices
Weapons would all be melted down
And we'd be safe in every town
I'm not religious but for what it's worth
Why can't we have Heaven here on Earth
Babies would be free from harm
Amusing everyone with their charm
Children could once more play outside
Without their parents by their side
Adults could go about their working day
With no fear of a bully coming their way
Pensioners would be looked after too
Cos everyone would care like me and you
People of all abilities would have a great time
Cos there'd be no such thing as hate crime
We'd all be living with a lot less stress
Cos the world just wouldn't be in this mess
We've all been born with a heart
And using it to care would be a good start
Reaching out a helping hand

Would soon catch on all over the land
No one on Earth would be a disgrace
No matter their religion... status or race
As long as they don't harm anyone
Who are we to tut at their life and fun
Changing the world shouldn't end in a fail
Our lives should be like a fairy tale
No ogres or witches or beanstalks in sight
Just a happy, safe place to live day and night
Ever since I was a little girl
That's how I've wanted to change the world.

Lynda George

WHY DID NOTHING GROW?

For months now we've all come to stare, yes stare with aching eyes
Searching, ever searching, from the start of each sunrise
It's autumn, we've passed the summer sun, rains kept up the river's flow
This year no leaves from trees will fall, oh why does nothing grow?

The fields were ploughed, the seeds were sown and fertiliser spread
And in a million urban gardens, a million manuals read
On pruning, turning compost, and planting seeds just so
The weather right, no frost at night, so why does nothing grow?

The earth looks rich, and is so dark, as far as Man can see
But no grass, no bush, no flower, no fruit upon the tree
The woods are quiet, no nests were built, no birds dash to and fro
Just a solitary starving squirrel, oh why does nothing grow?

Throughout the land the cattle die, killed for their stringy meat
The sheep, the deer, the rabbit, even dogs, as Man must eat
The world's begun to panic, as the food supplies run low
They've stopped the tests on nuclear bombs, perhaps now the crops will grow.

Pull down those power stations, spewing out their deadly waste
Let the buses, cars and lorries rot, on a final parking space
Take the super tankers off the sea then no discharged oil will flow
We must find a way to clean the air, perhaps then the crops will grow.

Let the world unite, its leaders meet, to join the latest race
Not for power or prestige, not for arms or ruling space

But a race to save this planet, before its last death throe
While we the people stand and stare, and pray the crops will grow.

Don Woods

NETWORK REPRISAL

I've realised that I stare at my phone a lot
With hopeful expectations of 'not a lot'
Time wasted, passing by, thoughts wondering, should I try?
Switching it off? Stepping outside?
No bars, no signal... time to abide?
Abide with what? Society's lies?
To tolerate and accept unanswered whys?
Politicians, the government, the media tries
To pollute and corrupt impressionable minds
Through technology and boxes of all different sizes
'Just switch on, plug in', but beware of their guises.
Facebook, the news, the bullshit peddlers
The lords and the ministers, the mindfuck meddlers.
The everyday someones, the you, mes but not thems
Us humans, us peoples, the ones they condemn
To a life full of servitude, without question of why?
Driven down and distracted by lights,
Tricked and cajoled so we forget why we fight.
By the men in their suits, with the world at their feet
Who trample us down with their lies and deceit.
So we call upon our human rights
The right to do nothing, just sit quiet and smile.
Wars waged for power and oil,
While the majority, the masses drown in their toil
For the world is indoctrinated by all of their spiel
Believe what I say, I dare you to 'feel'.
For me I simply can't do, the anger inside, the rage too real
For life could be simple, not made a big deal.
So why not switch off and unplug for a while?

Take stock of everything and open your eyes
Scream from the top of your lungs...
No more lies!

Andrew Ferguson

EXCUSES, EXCUSES

It's not that I am unconcerned
Please don't think that I don't care
Yes the world, it has its problems
I don't deny it and I am aware

Others can do so much better
And can do much, much more
Leave it to them who know best
And it will turn out right I'm sure

Believe me, I don't make excuses
This is not in any way a defence
But we will all soon see reason
And the world will follow sense

I am sure we all will soon see reason
For there are matters our rulers can't preside
When we dry the oceans and seas
And we have nowhere left to run and hide

It will never ever go that way
In times in history we do forget
I don't think it's time for panic
Do we really need drastic action yet?

My response is nothing new I'm sure
Your smile says you heard more than once before
If it helps I feel guilty and in a sense remorse
When our delusions have run their course.

History will be the judge, time decides
And the truth will out, it won't take long

Who was right and who was wrong?
It will be Mother Nature who presides.

I said but I'll say it again
I am one man, one man alone
And efforts will all be in vain
Can I make a difference on my own?

Look, I can see you are worried
But this world has seen a crisis or two
And it will keep on going and turning
Somehow we always come through.

Steve Prout

CHANGE THE WORLD

So - I'm going to be bold,
and say let's change the world.
I come home each night,
switch on the news and it gives me a fright.
I see disaster,
a world lost in its laughter.
From the top of my lungs I shout,
what do they have to laugh about?
They don't see the air,
polluted by the chemicals they spray on their hair.
They don't smell,
the trail of petrol supplied by the likes of Shell.
They don't fear the harm done to sweet nature,
an obligation - I believe on every creature.
I see a world lost in life,
unaware of environmental damage rife.
I see few groups voicing environmental concern,
yet so many others only bothered about what they earn.
Reporters reporting on apparent issues,
Yet - they turn a blind eye to the pile of tissues.
Things thrown around,
and still no one utters a sound.

So - I'm going to be bold,
and say together we can change the world.
Our leaders wave their hand,
but when it comes to voicing concern on air pollution -
environmental health - they bury their heads in sand.
Our friends having so much nightly fun,

throwing their leftovers under the sun.
When will the nation awake?
For sweet nature's sake.
To what do we owe,
the global warming show?
Do we not think we should do more?

So I'm gong to say let's all be bold,
and change the state of our world.

Aleena Faraz

THE LAND

Where do people go from the land
They go to the city for work
The same capital is at their backs
In their fight to survive

The land is my home
And at the same time
The land is a commodity
To be brokered by dealers

There is no altruism
In land management
What of Man?
Man is lost in the formula

The man is a silent witness
To the need of the commodity
That breaks men and women
On the journey of their lives

You live but what is living?
You procreate what are children
The living is lost in this
Lost to the need of land commodity

Who is it does not live
For fear of cold resignation
For fear of the cycle of living
For money abstracted in land

Money comes before people
People are nothing but money

It is not people who live
It is money which lives through people

They want to live for how long
They are a medium of life
There are bigger interests
Than the family of Man

If you go a long way
You come to land as capital
A superfluous population
The shades of the old world

The old people scratch a living
Those that are like them displaced
Scratch a living anywhere
Cynics laugh at their many efforts

The land is never waiting
The land gave up long ago
The men go into the land
The land never goes into the men.

Simon Warren

AS SOME WILL SWIM

When leading folk,
Some look for trends
Fashionistas. Just pretend?
To lead in life just can't be taught
Born a leader? There's a thought...
But born they are, and yet so few...
... Find ways to lead, and see it through
Rarer men are hard to find
Yet they possess a skill to bind
They hook you in,
Yet you're not caught
This rarest skill,
Lost armies sought
So what makes us mortals stand in line?
To grab a moment of their time?
Is it comfort, is it shelter?
As we hurtle down this helter-skelter...
All through time, men seek it out
The power of a leader's shout
A call to arms
A battle cry
Don't stand there, letting life drift by
But pick it up
Embrace its strength
Raise up from the gutter's stench
You have a choice, to join the throng
Own your mission, life it strong.
Or will you drift?
Far out to sea?

Lost.
Tormented.
Never free.
The choice is yours
Right in your hand
Drifting yields a life so bland
To drift suggests all passion waned
To follow brings a purpose gained
To change direction, when adrift
Requires that untold spirits lift
For men need strength to fight the tide
To find their way...
... A winning side
But most will drift
And never win
But take heart dear friend
As some will swim.

Kevin McCullough

THE HUMAN CURSE

Deforestation of the rainforest
To house cattle for McD's
Clear away the Amazon
So I can have a quarter pounder with cheese.

Can't get through the weekend
Without my McDonald's hangover cure,
Not worried that without enough trees
The planet's air will no longer be pure.

We need another mast in town,
To improve the speed of my Wi-Fi,
So I can get on the Daily Mail app
And read about the world's last rhino that died on Friday.

The planet is warming up but I think that's ace
The Maldives are slowly sinking
While I sip a pina colada catching rays on my face.

The world is about to flood
We will feel the force of the sea full pelt
Polar bears will be drowning,
As the icebergs displace and melt.

As I write these words I'm listening to the news,
The people of Syria
Are being gassed and being abused.
A nuclear war is being threatened by Kim Jong-un,
And another bomb has just been dropped
By someone linked to Osama Bin Laden.

While we throw these missiles of hate into the universe,
Mother Nature cringes at the effects of the human curse.
Rainbows, sunsets, paradise,
They were ours for us to take.
But we are slowly destroying them one by one,
With each and every mistake.

Lucy Harley

TECHNOLOGY

With technology comes advancement
Revolutions in research
Improving our efficiency
Utilising Planet Earth
Harnessing nature's bounty
Converting natural to man-made
Returning in an altered from
The ozone has to pay

Scientific investigations
Applied in innovative ways
Influencing complex issues
Thus, debates quite often raised
Beneficial to the future
Knowledge gained, endeavours made
What cost to unemployment
Vast machinery stealing wage

Communication made much easier
At expense of personal exchange
Screens now convey our message
Lost eye contact, talk seems strange
Transport sees development often
Gaining size, convenience, speed
Not for travellers these improvements
Money making human greed

Inventions in the medical world
Save countless lives for sure
But with mass-destruction weapons

Counteracted by each war
What objectives exploration
Sending billions into space
If disease, annihilation
Could endanger human race?

Environmental research
Over-population fears
Restoring Earth's resources
Burning money over years
Is technology all that's needed?
Can we save ourselves from us?
Use advancements for the better
Leave a world, not microdust

Nina Thilo

THE PARASITE

It seemed like just another harmless parasite -
A mutation of no consequence at all -
Essentially no different from all others
That infested Earth, some great, some very small.

But this was no mere minor irritation,
No modest infestation, like the rest.
This quickly proved itself to be malignant,
Behaving like a cuckoo in the nest.

Its predatory and voracious appetites
Preyed mercilessly on its lavish host,
And in spite of every effort to control it,
Ever more - and more - was what it wanted most.

It burrowed ever deeper for the nourishment
Demanded by its unrelenting greed,
Devouring and disfiguring, pursuing
Its own instinctive self-promoting creed.

Land, sea and air were equally its province
To invade and shape into its chosen scene.
When it looked beyond, for other worlds to plunder,
Its spore-like litter told where it had been.

The host's attempts to combat it all failed:
It survived attacks of famine, fire and flood,
And its own attempts at self-annihilation
Were nothing but the letting of some blood.

Its end is always in its own profligacy.
When Earth has given to it all it can,

The prolific parasite must surely perish
And Earth will then, at last, be cured of Man.

Alan Bignell

AN ECO-WITCH'S TASK

Amidst the brightest hours of day
When sun and normality hold sway
I watch and wait, hold tall and fast
Maintain the ruse till day is past

But darkness tells a different tale
In pure moonlight my spells won't fail
My beating heart is wild and clear
I work, and walk away from fear

No one knows the work I do
Searching hard to find the truth
To rid the world of all that's ill
Whilst others rest and slumber still

Night-time holds the greatest thrill
As I affirm my burning will
With heart afire and mind alive
I dance with elves, with dragons strive

To hold the Earth within my hand
And seek to heal the ravaged hand
To cleanse the seas, make pure the rain
So all Earth kind can breathe again

But commerce seeks to hold and bar
Defy the magic, dim the star
Finance rules without a care
And rips the world's resources bare

Men rage and rend and rape the world
The task is hard, the future furled

To hold the dream, the price I pay
Is ever to walk a lonely way

A single wish this night I make
Not for me but this world's sake
That I hold true to my heart's oath
To create a world of love and hope.

Lynne Emmerson

MATRICIDE

Is it not so, that we have fallen,
Almost deafened to 'the calling',
Our cenotaph, such great glass columns,
In the urban jungle sprawling.

Clouds drift ever up to meet the skies,
A blackened fog to blind the eyes,
And bind the throat and smother cries;
Such self-made smog forms our demise.

What of the sounds, at one time ringing?
For absent birds, we're want of singing,
Yet obvious to the pain we're bringing,
We continue the massacre, endless sinning.

Once majestic trees mastered the land,
Now raped to satisfy demand.
Is this the price we place on Man,
Are we worth more than the world we've damned?

How keen we are, our parts are played,
Without a thought to those betrayed.
We claim to know better, but still we degrade,
Though beauty for greed is an unequal trade.

Though nurtured by our earthly mother,
We drain the lifeblood of another;
An injustice which no excuse can cover,
Our heart's grown cold; we no longer shudder.

Is it too late to correct our mistakes,
To save the world we rend and break?

Let us open our eyes to what's truly at stake,
I pray we do soon; for all of our sakes.

Thea Pound

forward**poetry**

BIG HUNGRY TV

Press record on a big hungry TV.
Watch the moment -
People desperate,
Urban hell,
Protesting.
Vicious water shoves away
Their flags, posters.
What will we drink?
Police with helmets, shields -
Riot gear for this?

A country falls to ruins,
Banks borrowed too much,
Took from the people
Left them without,
A big angry finger jabs at their flag -
You owe us.
The people look on, sad.

Who are those poor on their farms over there?
Let's integrate them.
What is corn, what is bread?
They don't have a TV,
They don't have any wealth.

Parents work all day,
To pay
For the house, the car, the holiday,
Daughter's at home,
Alone,

Pressing record on a big hungry TV.
Watch the scenes, take it in.
Devours her face,
Her soul,
Makes her whole,
Shows her
This is how life is.

True lovers kept separate
To work like drones,
Find your profession, your place -
You're alone
In this world!
Make it count!
Towards what?
One day that big hungry TV
Will switch off.

Jessie Shier

SAVED TO SERVE

The good that I do is not by me,
No adoration and cheers do I deserve,
It's just that since Jesus set me free,
My life has been saved to serve.

When I feed the sick, help the poor,
Encourage and support my fellow man,
Remember Jesus did the same long before,
Now through me the Saviour does what He can.

All things come from Jesus' hand,
He suspends my soul from on high,
I am an instrument of good He's planned,
And I respond without asking why?

I am no saint or holy Joe,
Just a sinner who Jesus redeemed,
But when He calls I rise and go,
I was saved to serve or so it seemed.

But I am no robot without will,
I am born free to choose my way.
But I bow to Jesus and always will,
He is the purpose for my every day.

So don't thank the worker, I am like you,
I receive my reward from my heavenly boss,
And whatever I give and whatever I do,
He sees that I suffer no loss.

Saved to serve, to do what I can,
A conduit for my Saviour's love,

Heart to God and hand to Man,
Saved to serve sweet Jesus above.

Bill Hayles

CURTAIN FALL

As an unenlightened boy
Rooting and tooting
For shipyard workers in Gdansk
I never saw the other side
Of the curtain.

Only confusion for
The derisory remarks
Aimed at shot-putting women
And old men
In ill-fitting suits.

We only see
What they want us to see
It was the same for you
An Iron Curtain keeping citizens
Clean from Western stains.

Talking now it seems strange
That our childhoods were
Strikingly similar
Though your camps to
Black Sea vistas
Perhaps outshines
My youth hostelling
At Ambleside.

Serving our own country
Loyally and proudly
You at the Kremlin
Me with Strike Command

Both yearning to see
What the other was doing.

Now you travel freely here
And I travel freely there
Though now we are together
An impossible thought
All those years ago.

Perhaps it wouldn't
Have been the same
The wonder we still hold
As we share our stories
Of life's ups and downs
If we hadn't hid
For so long
Behind our curtains.

Gary Moss

HOW IS OUR EARTH?

How easy is it for us to know
The vulnerabilities of our planetary abode
Some gaze at nature through the kitchen window
The trees that blow, the grasses that grow
All signs that life is in motion and undertone
As foundation to what we as humans have exposed
Left prone a whole world where machines roam
Though to what degree of operational efficiency
Should be the question you and me
Reflect on when admiring our Earth's seamless harmony

How long will our wildlife survive
When economies seek to co-exist side by side
With factories built next to riverside and shorelines
Depriving what thrives for the sake of capitalised
Exploitation whose ultimate drive is an intangible lie
Money that only drains a society's need to utilise
Resources so that everyone benefits through equal divide
Instead of bankers levering extortionate sums
For corporations to stay high and dry in times
Of crisis when the poorest nations are forced into tonnes
Of debt that simultaneously arise
When the world is to no surprise
Together capable of feeding everyone on the horizon.

Matthew Western

THE SEA EMPRESS

June, the beach a jumbled mass of jetsam
Pearl riverlets adorn the sand sliding back
Towards the long abandoned weather hut
Footsteps through time had shaped this path

Seeds broadcast on the wind piloted here
Thrift, sea kale and Elijah Blue grass flourish
Clinging to the slopes that lead up to marram grass
Consuming the dunes with roots that bind

Winter gales shaped this comfortless bay
Summer visitors never mark time here
As a solitary fox slinks past ever looking
Rabbits bolt to nearby burrows safer now

Everywhere reminders of another life
Perched on the cliff face far behind
My father's house of stone, my house now
Extracted from this bleak and dismal bay

Looking out across this black track-marked bay
The Sea Empress split apart, disconnected
Each tide bleak, blacker than the last
Wave upon wave a procession of the dead

This turbid ebb and flow that greets me now
Where the sea meets this oil-black sand
Death's shadow left on this weathered shore
Through time will vanish and nature restore.

Edward Tapper

PLANET EARTH 2

The gift to the world has power beyond our contemplation,
It reveals a certainty of remarkable value, in its population,
Of which we must prize with pride and marvel at its credibility,
The scenery reveals a concept of beauty
Beyond one's visionary possibility.

It's breathtaking in its certainty of stature,
Wildlife and their discovery of natural habitat, thank you camera.
Captures the imagination into a feeling of wonder,
And fascination,
Incredible in their lives of habitat and strength,
Promotes adoration.

To finalise this remarkable programme,
The birds who display such artistry,
Displaying such rhythmic and artistic beauty in perfect harmony,
As if on parade for mere humans' pleasure, to admire and marvel,
This captivating dream of precision and sparkle.

This journey of discovery don't let it fade into oblivion,
It's a masterpiece of discovery and appreciation, a signalman,
An awakening to what we have on our great planet,
The magic of wisdom has been shared for our asset.

Lorna Tippett

A CRY FOR THE ENVIRONMENT

The environment needs to be tackled worldwide,
By combined work and effort by folk from all sides.
With pollution increasing day after day,
The future looks bleak and full of dismay.

Our high streets are littered and covered in gum,
Spat out by teenagers and an occasional mum.
Fine memorial seats burnt down in the park,
By hooligans who boast, "It's just for a lark."

Our rivers are choked with old junk and waste,
Thrown in by folk in too much of a haste.
They say, "Live for today, not for tomorrow"
Whilst those who care deeply are full of real sorrow.

We could all play our part to make our country clean,
Helping hands would work wonders to improve the scene.
Take time to clean up, put litter in the bin,
If we all pull together, I'm sure we could win.

This country would become such a beautiful place,
Make us proud to belong to the human race.
Visitors would enjoy our pristine green land,
And remember our heritage which is really grand.

Audrey Donoghue

IMAGINATION RUNNING WILD

Running wild and free
Behind me
From majestic mountains
Glaciers plough relentless to the bay.
Ahead gentle paths wind
Round fragrant meadows
To golden sands and clear blue sea
Where yachts,
Sails pink in the sunset,
Drift to anchor
Against the palm-fringed islands.

Alas wishful thinking
And so not so
Just Crag Hill
No grand and rocky fell
No Lakeland peak or limestone plain
Just bog
Sloping steeply
To muddy summit and lonely cairn.

A fell runner's dream
Two miles down
Glorious descent
Racing, chasing, roaring.
Soft yielding ground.
No people,
No erosion,
No rocks to catch the feet
Or twist the limbs,

No need to think, just free to run,
Uncrowded and easy.
Deserted enough to run naked
And lose no self respect.

My body here, running and alone.
But in wild imagination
I am anywhere
Doing anything
With anyone.
With or without clothes.
But I actually like it here.

Garry Rowlands

FULL CIRCLE

First of us was Hub,
solid core, the heart of us.
Then Spokes, radiating,
a star sniffing at infinity.
Last was Rim, binding
all to the wheel.

Together we made the world small,
set men free from the scourge
of unsatisfied appetite.
We filled bellies and empty minds,
fed the vacuum that was imagination.
We gave you the gift of idleness,
made you king of the animals,
watched as you prayed to the god
of the unnecessary.

How quickly we grew,
gobbling up invention,
carrying men from fields of corn
to fields of blood.
Our tracks covered the world,
trampled the sanctuaries where nature
cowered from our strength.
We watched as you sucked the juices
from the fat fruit of Earth,
spitting out pips with a glutton's glee.

Listen to us now!
Hear the creak of an un-oiled wheel.

See the carriage moving,
its load shrouded in black.
And behind the mourners,
see how thin they are,
old eyes filled with a new fear.

John Plevin

OUR CHANGING WORLD - THERE NEVER SEEMS TO BE ANY

Our world has become a more dangerous world
So much trouble and strife we have to face
Climate change brings threats of overheating
Unexpected electoral candidates their rivals are beating
This world is now full of unprecedented surprises
As one after another a new threat to world peace arises.

Leaders rise and fall
Sometimes it's a very close call
We worry what changes they will bring
Did we indeed vote for the right thing?
Each day we wake to something new
Then days later the outcome we sadly rue.

Peace and stability are on a knife's edge
As I look hesitantly over my window ledge
I too don't know which way I should turn
But I know what I as a pensioner earn
Won't buy me very much
Come on you politicians you're way out of touch.

You're here to make changes to our daily lives
Listen to the pleas of young and old, husbands and wives
For it seems that all we do is go round in rings
And no contentment to the world it brings.

Patricia J Tausz

MOTHER NATURE'S FURY

The trees have been replaced by flats;
The animals adorn our walls
On widescreen TVs, richly coloured,
To view them one and all.
We gawp at distant foreign lands;
Pretend they're not the same,
To save ourselves embarrassment,
And re-direct the blame.
We tell ourselves they're different,
From us and what we eat,
While lounging somewhere comfortable
In artificial heat.
The man, he said: "When brushing teeth,
Take care to turn off taps."
So now I'm saving planets
While killing pesky ants
Who make their nests in flower beds
Without the thought for time or cost
I spent in making my displays;
On them, the point is lost.
I want to make a better world,
By any way or means,
And would have found out how by now,
If not for glowing screens.

When Mother Nature's fury comes,
And serves a dish that's cold and sweet,
I hope we've words of our regret
While holding our receipt.

Harry Husbands

GREEN TEARS FOR THE OZONE

Cloud hangs low, wrapped around the trees
a day for dreams, yet wakened ghosts still weep
drifting through time, reaching for pole position
hard to break through, too scared of superstition.

Spells of desire, form from spoken word
fall from the page breathed into air
gently poisoned by traffic fumes
stealth is the hand that spreads the gases
there is no protective mask or purifier.

Slow and silent, airborne poison moves, invisibly,
Abandonment of societal responsibility
who is protecting the vulnerable
from that which they cannot see?
'Take the money' and let the engines roar.

The future stolen from the young
to fill the coffers of 'the one'
bereft, the sleepers wrest with death
our guardians, of the petrol heads
deflated, still no longer ill
hemlock toxins in the fumes
life in ruins, breath to rest
lay your head down, wake no more
sleep on the pillow, of the leafy floor.

Jackie Roberts

THE BLAME GAME

Rain on rain, sun on sun,
Melting away what was once one,
Hot to cold and cold to hot,
Over time what will be forgot?
As blizzards rage and heat soars,
What will be left when the ocean roars?

Will our skies be clear or sooty and grey?
Will the polar bears leave or remain the same?
And fewer in number will all beings be,
And fingers point at you and at me.

And flying about are answers indeed,
To the tricky questions that might be perceived,
Telling us all to act with caution and speed.
But how fast is this coming 'global warming' it's called,
Debate politicians as scientists scald.

Our Paris Agreement that was stumped right there,
By the American man with fake blonde hair.
And another attempt might the high and mighty make,
To stop the Earth from losing its stake.
In the constellations and planets of which we call space,
Yet it seems our world is poisoned, by none but the human race.

Chloe Edwards-Calvert

CULPABILITY

Neck craned, I squint, tracking
silhouettes against blueness,
chevrons of silent migrants
hitchhiking your borderless world.

High enough to abstract Earth,
you sail another sphere of existence
in sanctuary above this
beautiful, teetering planet.

One foot in, one out, we've
orphaned ourselves from nature.
Evolution's intended or failed guardian?
Here, at least, to bear witness.

How bleak a world without birds.
How paltry our landscape and poetry.

Untangling your wings and feet
little sparrow, you eyed me with innocent
indifference. No fond gaze returned
my slow, reverent cradling.

Such delicate beauty,
softness belying a precise
feathering honed by aeons of
nature's randomness.

Little sparrow, you dodge my
rapacity and nature's rawness.
Your paradise would have no place for me
but mine would be bereft without you.

Kate Thick

SENDING ALL OUR LOVE
(22.5.17 Manchester Arena bombings)

Another morning woken with a clear mind
To find social media screaming
Another heart-wrenching terrorist attack
Targeted at the young and innocent
Tears stream our face
The realisation is mortifying
As we wonder in our heads is this world safe?
And in our hearts, that gut-wrenching ache
You can feel the pain and fear
And it's terrifying and saddening to hear
Someone so young lose their life
Before it even began
So much innocence when life is full of laughter
And times like these are the fun memories that should live on
Taken away, replaced by so much sorrow
So much love sent their way, touched our hearts
And through fear and pain brought together people
But never can it take back this horror
Never can it replace that beating heart
That beautiful soul
With love, with sympathy
We pray to the heavens
These angels rest in peace
Never forgotten.

Danielle Harris

A WORLD OF TWO HALVES

We have people on the streets
We have people with empty bellies
We have people with not a penny
Whilst others have fancy tellies.

We have people without hope
We have people in despair
We have people with tattered clothes
Whilst the rest don't seem to care.

We have people who are rich
We have people who are poor
The gulf between the two
It widens more and more.

We have gluttony and greed
We have hunger and poverty
We have people so in need
Whilst the rest refuse to see.

We have disparity of wealth
We have waste whilst others starve
Oh what an unjust world
With two unequal halves.

We have sick that go untreated
We have children go unfed
We spend more on wars and weapons
We have masses that are dead.

We have a world in turmoil
We have a world that cries
Will someone please just comfort
Our world before she dies.

Anthony David Beardsley

NATION S

In the silence of the night
I had the strangest dream
That God had asked me to unite
The nation for his theme

To stop the murder and strife
To end the endless grief
To throw away the bloodstained knife
And find a peace to keep

To help his people understand
Each other's different ways
And show them that the promised land
Was well within their gaze

So enormous was the task
It weighed upon my mind
And yet the question must be asked
How could I save mankind?

I called the leaders to my side
And asked them if they knew
Of rules by which they could abide
To which they could be true.

Each one gave his version
Of what had best be done
But no one knew for certain
Or trusted anyone.

They argued back and forth at length
I gave up in despair

It seems mankind will never learn
To treat his neighbours fair.

Robert Stevens

LOOKING BACK

Looking back at what
How the government didn't fix people's lives
How they just thought about themselves
We are all selfish to the core
It's human nature and fun
In the festive dream of kingdom come

Looking back and what for
The same old broken promises
We have won and lost
We have opened our mouths
And what have we said
Some are alive
And some are dead

Live life and don't get depressed
It's okay for some
It's hard for others
Looking back, looking forward
Can we do things better next year
We will see it when it comes

The Christmas rush
The new year get-together
We are a little older
We have good health
Be positive, live in love
Whatever words mean to you
Try and help somebody
And stop being selfish

Looking back in the past
In the present and future
In space and time.

Kenneth Mood

IT WASN'T ME

It wasn't me.
I didn't poison your rivers
and kill your fish, I wasn't
there when the last red squirrel
left, I only chopped down
your trees to build a fire
when I was cold.

It wasn't me
who tinkered with your crops
and played God with the food
you gave us - not me,
not me at all.

My friends did it,
took more,
much more
than I did and no one's
blaming them, it wasn't
just me, it's not
my fault and anyway
there's loads
left, what's
the fuss?

If bees are dying
why blame me? You know
I'd never touch them, I wouldn't
harm a fly, what's all
the fuss about?

I'm only doing
the same as everyone else,
Why pick
on me?

Why are you looking
at me
like that?

Don't blame me.

Diana Devlin

HEAL THE WORLD

If I could plant the dying trees of the world
And stop them from falling to the ground
To change the world and make it a better place
For you and for me

If I could pour the water into lakes and oceans
And stop the floods in countries from afar
To change the world and make it a better place
For you and for me

If I could build the highest mountain in the land
And stop all the deaths and dooms of the world
To change the world and make it a better place
For you and for me

If I could protect the weakest deer of the world
And prevent hunters from seeking their prey
To change the world and make it a better place
For you and for me

If I could give everyone a comfortable home
And make them feel loved and respected
To change the world and make it a better place
For you and for me

I would do it all.

Doris K Williams

LIFE AFTER EARTH

Space travellers moving curiously around ancient Andromeda,
In cigar-shaped ships of silver magic,
Quietly in a weightless heaven
Scanning a planet that died.
Back to a time when Earth was bursting with life
Aqua blue and forest green
Now a distant memory and haunted by images
Smoking plumes of death and destruction
War and famine and desperation
People frozen in time amid rags and oblivion,
Scanning now the history books,
Images of men in caves
Images, flashes, pictures and words
Images of villages, towns and cities
Images of vehicles on wheels.
Books and primitive computers
Bejewelled kings and queens now buried in dust.
Children of the robot encased in metal pods.
They don't seek the earth beneath their feet
Or dream of swimming in the oceans where life began
But cradle their lost souls
Pilgrims on a new path.

Julie Spackman

PLASTICITY

The party was advancing too fast into my lair
horizon pulsating in numbers not easy to compare.
I quickly climbed the safety stairs to lock myself away
I could not face the horror of an entourage array...

Out front there was a leader, swaying, plunging forth,
followers spread about him from east, south, west and north.
I trembled in my prison watching the advance
such an army huge and powerful, would I stand a chance?

I knew there was no answer, to stop them was too late,
all the stupid errors, a mass of spin of fate.
Everyone responsible, none would admit defeat,
facing a huge black hole syndrome, not easy to beat...

Caretakers of the world did not all unite,
waste of wars and terrorism not easy to fight,
as the advancing army of plastics pushing in its wake
holds the life and soul of a world left to *undertake*...

Meg Lewis

IF YOU HAVE A NEIGHBOUR

You too are a neighbour,
in a genuine, if not vivacious district.
Soap operas' fictional areas labour
to be more vivid than yours - less morally strict.
Remember, they're not real; those happenings are vamped
by actors in ersatz homes - where they've only camped.

Estate agents' property descriptions are
silent about human contents of adjoining
dwellings, because nearness to friends could mar
movers' prospects of empathy, and social joining.
Hospitality seen on TV's over-rated -
Long gone are the days when neighbours were related.

If elderly widowers, or widows had been
in hospital, their neighbours took turns to ensure
their homes were warm, and they had hot dinners daily.
Few get such care in Dorking or Rayleigh.
Young families' lives come first, not Mrs Next Door.

Gillian Fisher

A SPITEFUL HAND

The golden threads and hidden webs surround
Each living thing, and all things dead on Earth
From dawn of time to setting of its day
The golden threads remain beyond all age.
And yet each passing parasite still tries
To cut and slice and tear the webbing down
And Mother Nature trembles and keeps score
Until the web is fragile, then she moves
With earth and fire and wind and savage rains
She will regain her world and wipe it clean.
We build to weather all her perfect storms
We think her cruel and heartless in her reign
And yet she asks us nothing for her world
Except the time and care to thread the eyes
Of needles spun with whiskers and with light
To soothe the scarring lands and heal the skies.
The golden threads will be here when we're gone
Our legacy will be healed wounds or scars.

Tia-Louise Way

THE CAPITAL

A groaning throne of tough steel supports the
boss, fat from the spoils of the street below.
Gazing through the office-glass, he smirks at
the city he thinks he has conquered.
At the summit of success, he fiddles,
as hazy smog falls on the city skyline.

Beneath him, London dissolves from terraced to
detached, to concrete slabs of council flats.
Kettles on and phones withdrawn as Ben strikes twelve -
"Those social parasites should find some work!"
splutters the digital chorus, spewing
hot coffee and bile over plastic desktops.

Scraps are thrown to a fortunate few as
connivers conduct the capital's song.
"It's hard to see," says the boss at the top,
"how the city's song is possibly wrong."

Edward Fernyhough

GLOBAL WARMING

Climate change is real
Though sadly not believed
Have you not observed
The changes
To the world around us
Extremes in weather
Where once was snow
Now heavy rain and floods
More droughts and fires
Our seasons so different now
The Earth's temperature
Melting the snow and ice
Land eroding, vanishing
Before our eyes
Animals' lives at risk
So many endangered or extinct
Our lives impacting
On our world
Travel, central heating, pollution
Causing so much devastation
Oceans in peril
Overfishing, habitat loss
Dumped rubbish generating mayhem
Sea levels rising
Waters warming
Mammals struggling to survive

When will we wake up
To the changes that are real

For our future generations
Will you act now?

Lady Gail Underwood

A LETTER AFTER

Dear Cassandra,
Your voice is hard and shrill
And raving with tumultuous things.
I can hear none of the birdsong when you speak,
Nor the breeze, nor those distant waves that
So far off, lose their thrash and become a gentle echo.
Why is your voice not soft as the world is?
Why must you drown a room so permanently
And make an enemy of reality?

Dear Cassandra,
The day is hot and dry, where darkness
Yields no relief from the monster,
Even with those teeth of the sea gnashing so nearby.
The sun taunts us to greet them, to relent
As a welcome end, like a rat pressed against a stomach.

You cut the thread between hope
And fear, and brought us only one.
You soaked the land in dread
Where you should have made us listen.

Joseph G Lay

THE CURE

"The world needs to change
It's diseased and dying
Each day it worsens
But the government aren't trying..."

These are the words
That echo through the breeze,
That bounce off the oceans,
And rustle through the trees.
From the mouths of the people
Who claim that they care.
The ones who take lifts
Instead of the stairs.
Who drive to a store
Half a mile down the street.
Who stare at their phones
And eat too much meat.
So yes, change is needed,
But not just in industries.
The change is required
Within you and me.
We're more than just one person
We're an army for good,
So start making some changes
Or prepare for the flood.

Emma Duggan

THE WORLD NEEDS A SAGE

Out here, with the birds, the bees, the grass and the air, I'm safe
Like two koala bears on an eucalyptus tree swinging for fun
Red and yellow spotted socks are pruned to match my feet
A ladybird hits the snooze alarm to wake me from sleep
Mother Nature's tentacles ignite a passion that makes me numb
Senseless, the deprivation borrows jealousy to follow patterns
Sordid regress, spatula screwed to cyan mouths
Clink goes titanium, to butter the brow of famine
Selfish contained gestures, who needs to reach out with venom?
While the bile slurs the stomach juice, you'll be eaten in two
Looking for a rescue, a way out, or escape
Such dangers lurk in innocence, the world swaps change for sage.

Liba Ravindran

BE RESPONSIBLE

There are many people, who accept dirty streets and parks,
To kick and throw rubbish around is seen as just a lark!
Responsibility, nobody wants, while squalor reigns,
After picnics al fresco, wrapping and cartons remain.

Old newspapers are dropping on the ground and I call it a sin
Because on every road, I can see there is a bin.
If we adults as one, take care of the day-to-day stuff,
Would protect the look of the local area - fear it's not enough.

For too long, people have on others tried to put the blame,
Use excuses for selfish behaviour - it is lame.
If we all aim to keep tidy our roads and green spaces,
Our environment would be better for the human race.

Sue Mullinger

AMAZON PAIN FOREST

You may look at the sea of trees,
Majestic, striding across the land
Reaching towards the purest air.
But no one can see
The sleight of hand
As onlookers stare.

They feel the agony
Of the tree falling.
They hear its final sound
But no one can truly feel
The most appalling
Noise as it hits the ground.

The habitat lost forever,
As our greed takes hold
And forgets about this Eden.
But no one wants to see
The secrets richer than gold
Hidden in the Amazon's garden.

For all the eyes looking backwards
Are searching for needed answers.
But no one wants to see anymore
The loss of one of nature's treasures.

Andrew Elze

SIGN OF THE TIMES

What is this life when unemployed?
What can we do to fill the void?
More time to go and walk the dog
Escaping from the city smog.

More time to sample nature's ways
To go up on the hills and laze.
But though we've time to stand and stare
Our wildlife is becoming rare.

And as I rest beneath the bough
I see no ruminating cow.
Because they're in a massive shed
Where they are milked and they are fed.

And modern farming, it is clear
Makes trees and hedges disappear.
So where can little creatures hide
When Man sprays with his pesticide.

I see no shepherd - see no flock -
Why can't we just turn back the clock?

Jonathan Bryant

POETRY'S NEW DAWN

A new dawn of poetry has just arrived,
And I am the rising sun,
Its popularity low and deprived,
But now the new era has begun,
Readers will experience all my work has to mention,
Becoming the characters in every story,
From rhyming attitude to verbal vengeance,
Standing at the start line of my forthcoming glory,
Soon I will become your new fascination,
When the poetic world rolls to my feet,
I will be the author of your imagination,
Everything I write, your lips will repeat,
No more poems about the flowers and birds,
Only what I create shall be mentioned,
And from your bitten tongue will come the words,
"I have just read the work of a legend"!

Ian McNamara

VIEW OF CHANGE

Dear Scotia, will your islands and highlands
Still be a view, a year from now
Or will we see, malnourishment of despair
A bad manner of disregard by
The secretary of state, like a beggar, they won't bat an eye
My glass will run dry, due to the crisp in the air,
The golden drink fit for a god will vanish like dinosaurs
Lands I once walked upon fade away
beneath my damp feet
Our joy of snowflakes will turn blind,
My kin will never see, as I once did
The sun will burn and battle down like a thousand slashes,
Blood will land, a drop at a time
You, me and our government are at fault!
We were blind, but now we can see
A vision ahead called *change*.

Calum Higgins

INNOVATION

It's deprivation,
In school it's just evaluations,
They pass on the information,
Cause a complication,
Confuse the conversation,
Heated issues, call the fire station,
But there's people in starvation,
They're in desperation,
We gotta help with motivation,
It's not another vacation,
It should be a loving invitation,
With a bit of improvisation,
We could change a nation,
And help the human creation,
In this situation,
There ain't no hesitation,
Complete the love equation,
Give the world a great sensation,
Plan an organisation,
Take a flight to our destination,
And invade their minds with inspiration!

Annum Mahmood

EARTH

The world will evolve, with or without us,
as it always has, and always will.
But we can help slow our own decline
if we conserve, instead of kill.

Ice ages come and ice ages go,
and global warming is nothing new.
If we are to both survive and thrive
we need to change our blinkered view.

We need to harness nature's power,
not destroy forests that give us life,
nor increase pollution for profit's sake...
our future sits on the edge of a knife.

It's beyond belief some leaders ignore
experts' advice on our planet's state.
All we can do is petition and hope
common sense returns before it's too late.

Tracy Davidson

ACID RAIN

Rainfall of gases from hell
Robbing us of peace
Who will ring the bell?
For it to cease

Exploring oil from here
Gas flaring our skin and soul
Prayers for us to be out there
Without pollution toll

Our environment is polluted
By the spill of oil rigs
The Niger Delta is not saluted
They should stop treating us like pigs!

We cannot eat dead fish in the sea
Some indigenes were silenced by genocide
Government proposal like a pea
No choice; nowhere else to reside

Who will change our world?
Some activists died fighting our battle
With words sharper than the sword
Rest in peace without a rattle.

Funmi Oyewole

LIFE

I am Planet Earth,
soul supplier of the sustenance you need.
A reluctant resource to be plundered
to satisfy human greed.

I am the vast ocean,
flooded with tears of grief
for the many lives taken
by each thoughtless, thankless thief.

I am the sun,
that warms and burns bright.
My sister is the tranquil moon,
who reflects a gentler light.

I am the air;
I am the breath of life.
I am the wild wind
that cuts like a knife.

I am a woman, I am not divine.
I am not an angel, but just one of humankind.
I am a human being with the right to be;
I am a living being with the right to be me.

Mary Chapman

UNTITLED

Are we a nation who has lost its way
Wandering on an uncertain island
Washed by waves of foaming dissent
Tossed on foaming, fearsome seas?

Have we become a people that dwells
On past conquests and exploits,
Reliving victories and successes
Past history presented in bite-size chunks?

Do we turn our backs on poverty
The young man busking in the street
The family without enough to eat
The homeless young girl sleeping rough?

We are a nation of a blessed country
Yet sometimes we admit in the privacy of home
To hearing vulpine howls at night
And discordant voices wanting change.

Caroline Buddery

SHIFTING TIDES

Sea level variants
Flux and form flotillas
Under ice caps
Or equators
Or barrier reefs.

To edge sea plates, like fluttering foamed fingers
Touching, smoothing, changing torrents
Shifting, sliding surreptitiously
Slinking nearer a maritime
Natural disaster

Collapse

Into a tragic sinkhole
As the world
Gyrates
On a volatile axis
Folds into an exhausted blood orange
Bled dry inertia
Stenching rot and corruption
Deadly wars

Evaporating into potential nihilism
A senseless collapse, tectonic plates shattered
Into a broken nothingness.

Tracy Allott

THE WORLD TODAY

Evolution created a wonderful world
Amazing, spectacular things unfurled.
Which are gradually being destroyed it seems
By the march of technology and entrepreneur dreams.
Trains and cars, yes are great
We are now being destroyed with pollution they make.
Our natural habitats are dwindling fast
Where our wildlife thrived, but no longer last.
Without the flowers and shady trees
There's nowhere to go for our birds and bees.
All playing their part in the wheel of survival
Their contribution just has no rival,
Pollinating plants, distributing seeds
To produce the crops for our everyday needs.

Audrey A Allocca

THE CALIMA

A heavy warmth penetrating,
In a claustrophobic shell;
Movement is abated,
Praying for a breeze to quell.

A breath difficult to take,
Tormented by the atmosphere;
No relief in its wake,
Ingested lungs won't clear.

This heavy Calima,
The Sahara is to blame;
Dust settling won't redeem her,
Only cleaner winds can tame.

The cloud clings to the island,
Like a predator or stalker;
The mist not letting go,
Until a gust has caught her.

Praying for a shift,
A storm to remove,
Quell and bring a lift,
Out of this perpetual groove.

Christine Carol Burrows

JENGA

When did they last spot a tiger in the wild?
What had driven the seagulls inland?
Why are the ice caps melting?
Where has the ozone layer gone?
How many plant species has our planet lost?
Who is going to bring us crashing down?

The answer, my friends, is written in ourselves,
As piece by piece do we, blindfolded by our greed
And deluded by our conceited beliefs,
Strip this dear green place of its rich variety
Until one day we will lay bare its skeleton,
Which will then crack to crash around us.

If Man is taken as the measure of all,
Such pride will cause our final fall.

Denis Bruce

PAYBACK

Man has grossly mistreated you
We're steeped you in poisons and gases galore
Yet you provide such natural beauty
That keep our kind in awe.
We don't deserve your pleasures
We just keep chipping and hacking away
And the problem with this selfishness
Is that one day we are going to pay.
Our distorted paradise is a right picture
Full of towers and concrete blocks
It's not the green place it once was
It's suffered so many bumps and knocks.
The ozone layer is declining
Problems bigger every year
Global warming and pollution
Are choking our precious Earth.

Donna McCabe

DEAD STREAM

Struggling along an overgrown bank
Path with nettles and ragwort, rank,
Came upon a turgid stream
Slow moving water with duckweed green.

Slime and scum at water's edge
Hanging in strings from dying sedge,
Filthy water, barely seen
Under oily blue iridescent sheen.

Bubbles of gas escape from the bed
Dying stream, almost dead
No vole, or coot or dragonfly
Nothing of beauty to please the eye.

Man killed the stream with his pollution
And Man alone holds the solution,
For in his quest for easy wealth
He thinks of nothing but himself.

Ken Capps

THE NATURAL WORLD

I love the smell of rain
And the heat before a storm.

I love the sound of a thunder clap
And the coming of the dawn.

I love the warmth of the sun,
And the relief of a cool breeze.

I love the smell of flowers
And the strength of the trees.

I love the sound of my dog's bark
And the meow of next door's cat.

I love steep green hills
And fields that are flat.

I love the natural world
And I think we need to help it.

We should take better care
Because we couldn't live without it.

Cher Clee

THE PRECIOUS LIFE AND HOW IT STARTED

Our human form,
And magical creations,
Change the world to make us all one.
From the power of love
Can take over the bad.
Hypnotised the sad to make them feel glad.
Cure the good
Help the innocent child grow
With water and food.
Open that hole.
Corruption swallowed up,
Melt it away with a powerful thrust.
The picture of beauty keep us healthy
Love and honour
Kindness not greed.
Love our neighbour
And all creations
The beauty, the power.
Sweet smells of aroma
Living cells
Ringing bells.

Shirley Walsh

BLIND

The world seems to see in black and white
No compromise and that's just not right

Death, war and destruction
There is no happy deduction

What is our fate
Is it all just hate?

There seems to be no love shared
Our teeth are always bared

We show no mercy, we just kill, kill, kill
Is it the red or the blue pill?

It's not just humans, animals die too
At our hands, we just haven't got a clue

Will the world ever change
Or are we all in the shooting range?

Cath Harker

THE POEM CALLED UNTITLED

Tuning into intuition getting to know ourselves in life's mission,
taking a stand whilst having something to stand for that's already
sought by our soul that knows the decision
so this is for me as it is you too, to see if we can see this through
one love as we live as one just speaking truth
they say the old wisdom is lost, maybe it's just long overdue and if
that's not the case at least we have the ability to make new,
so if you do take anything from this, just know by choice we can
always change the world if we choose

Dane Bancroft

EDIBLE GARDENS

Start an edible garden in a size to suit
Nothing better than fresh seeing a root
There are so many seeds for you to grow
Planting them and caring easy to follow
Watching the seeds become plants
Taking care of them, keep away the ants
Growing is cheaper, healthier, why not
All the family can join in the same spot
Tasty carrots, cabbage, spinach, onions to go
Mix and chop herbs and stir with the flow
Fun fitness and family together time
Healthy meals and snacks galore
Could anyone wish for more?

Kelly Stevens

ACCOMPLISH... OR DO NOT BEGIN?

To accomplish - you have to have passion;
To have passion - you have to believe;
To believe - you have to care;
To care - you have to have empathy;
To have empathy - you have to understand;
To understand - you have to have patience;
To have patience - you have to be calm;
To be calm - you have to be at peace;

Peace, understanding, passion - especially passion -
Will help you accomplish many things.
Without these attributes is it better not to begin
Or rather, better to fail than not to try?

Judy Rochester

BRAVE NEW WORLD

Oh brave new world,
What a beautiful place,
A pity you're infested by the human race!

Oh brave new world,
You brought forth grace,
Only to have it tainted by the human race!

Oh brave new world,
You're a terminal case,
Due to the ignorance of the human race!

Oh brave new world,
You die at a tremendous pace,
Raped and pillaged by the human race!

Oh brave new world,
Will you leave no trace?
After you have been destroyed by the human race!

Lawrence Sharkey

CHANGE THE WORLD

O to change the world.
But how?
By getting rid of evil doers in the world.
But how?
By planting lots of oxygen giving, cobo absorbing trees all over the
World.
But how?
By farming forests and protecting the lung green trees all over the
World.
But how?
By loving humanity and following church doctrine all over the
World.
But how?
By love of the world for then with all this done and redesign,
Invention
The world will be a new more intelligent world.
Moving on to wow!

Keith William Newing

EARTH SINGS

If Earth sings
What song would she sound?

A last lament
For wilderness lost
And dying coral seas?

The strident anthem
Of human industry
And Science's advance?

A joyful dance
For each mother's love
And hopeful birth?

Or bitter cries
For suffering Man
Of hunger, thirst and war?

If Earth sings
Her complex song
Tells of these and more
The music swells
As if to say
Regard this Earth with awe.

David Wilson

COOMBE HILL

I sit at the summit and observe a kestrel
Hovering for prey on the eddies of the air
The sky is an azure blue
Not a cloud on the horizon
On this bright spring day
Only a slight breeze swaying the branches
Of the oak trees

The view is a patchwork quilt of fields
Golf courses and church spires
An inanimate monument sits on top of the hill
To the inane Boar War

But Coombe Hill is a monument
To beauty over a cruel and bloody conflict.

Mutley

UNTITLED

We are Britain, we are bold
Here we live, the young and the old
Different religions, different races.
But did you see their sad, sad faces?
We will cry, we'll shed a tear
But no to the terrorists, you're not welcome here.
We're not scared, we're not afraid
You bring us hurt, you bring us pain.
But here we stand, our hearts remain,
We'll stand up tall and we'll show our pride,
Together we stand and remember that night.

Victoria Jeffery

CHANGE THE WORLD

What if
We could change the world one step at a time?
What if
We made someone who is sad, happy?
What if
We pick up other people's rubbish one bag a day?
What if
We helped that lady with the heavy shopping?
What if
We all planted a tree each day?
What if
We all gave up meat?
What if
We all grew proper food?
What if
We each house a homeless person?
What if
We all start with one small step?

Sam Hill

BRAITHWAITE BRIDGE COLLAPSED!

Rain came down, wild wind wild
River run out of control
Four to five feet of water!
Bringing mud, silt and twigs tree branches.
Rushing towards the arch of the bridge
Tarmac loosen, cemented brick loosen
Into the river!
Brick by brick fall into mud
Silt and clay, twigs, branches
Roots flow by emptiness.
What happened to the bridge?
Where is the bridge?
Rain, more rain, wild wind wild
Bridge swept away!

Martin F Holmes

CIRCLE OF LIFE

Life inside of me, growing, existing, being.
A little part of me,
A little part of you,
His own part too.
While one life delivers,
Another must go.
The balance is important,
Death and life both show.
He is here,
But you are not,
Your presence remains near,
I shall not fear.
Life will come and life will go
Take comfort, we have love
The next step we will never know.

Faye Lucas

HOLD IT CLOSE

Beauty is best when it is protected
And we know, each of us,
How to exhibit, carefully, a rose.
Same with our environment.
This life-giving planet, this delicate Earth.
If we don't hold it close caringly,
We may bring destruction to our doorsteps...
We might summon our own end:
A procession of coffins, dug graves,
Burial alive in water or fire.

Muhammad Khurram Salim

DID YOU KNOW EACH FLOWER HAS A SECRET JUICE - THE MYSTERY OF LIFE

Dewdrops have the power to heal,
Roses are the flower for skin,
Lilac is the flower of love.
Foxgloves are so soft, if one had to sleep forever
It would be on their touch.
Each time you pick a flower,
Give a thought to their inner self,
For God put his secret of life just inside
For you to share
And find happiness within yourself.

Barbara Posner

PRESENT DAY

Welcome to present day;
The sky is polluted and the ground is grey
Humans have learnt to mass produce their prey
This is called farming.

Wild animals that tame ourselves
Hunting meat off Tesco shelves
Travelling tarmac roads to skyscrapers
That scrape the sky away.

Jake Yates

FINALLY

Tomorrow has arrived
Leaving the sadness of yesterday in its wake
The sunshine dances on your lips
As I catch a wry smile on your face
In your slumber you pull me closer
And we drift off into our dreams... encased in happiness
And bathed in love... forever...

Paula Greene

HUNTER GATHERER

We will come to you in the end
On our hands and knees,
To worship at the altar of nature.
When money has become worthless
Cars are chunks of useless rusting metal,
And all the technology in the world
Hasn't saved our sorry ass.

Nigel Bangert

FORWARD POETRY INFORMATION

We hope you have enjoyed reading this book - and that you will continue to enjoy it in the coming years.

For free poetry workshops please visit **www.forwardpoetry.co.uk**. Here you can also subscribe to our monthly newsletter.

Alternatively, If you would like to order further copies of this book or any of our other titles, then please give us a call or log onto our website.

Forward Poetry Information
Remus House
Coltsfoot Drive
Peterborough
PE2 9BF

(01733) 890099